Endorsements for the Church Questions

"Christians are pressed by very real questions. How does Scripture structure a church, order worship, organize ministry, and define biblical leadership? Those are just examples of the questions that are answered clearly, carefully, and winsomely in this new series from 9Marks. I am so thankful for this ministry and for its incredibly healthy and hopeful influence in so many faithful churches. I eagerly commend this series."

R. Albert Mohler Jr., President, The Southern Baptist Theological Seminary

"Sincere questions deserve thoughtful answers. If you're not sure where to start in answering these questions, let this series serve as a diving board into the pool. These minibooks are winsomely to-the-point and great to read together with one friend or one hundred friends."

Gloria Furman, author, *Missional Motherhood* and *The Pastor's Wife*

"As a pastor, I get asked lots of questions. I'm approached by unbelievers seeking to understand the gospel, new believers unsure about next steps, and maturing believers wanting help answering questions from their Christian family, friends, neighbors, or coworkers. It's in these moments that I wish I had a book to give them that was brief, answered their questions, and pointed them in the right direction for further study. Church Questions is a series that provides just that. Each booklet tackles one question in a biblical, brief, and practical manner. The series may be called Church Questions, but it could be called 'Church Answers.' I intend to pick these up by the dozens and give them away regularly. You should too."

Juan R. Sanchez, Senior Pastor, High Pointe Baptist Church, Austin, Texas

"Where can we Christians find reliable answers to our common questions about life together at church—without having to plow through long, expensive books? The Church Questions booklets meet our need with answers that are biblical, thoughtful, and practical. For pastors, this series will prove a trustworthy resource for guiding church members toward deeper wisdom and stronger unity."

Ray Ortlund, President, Renewal Ministries

Who's in Charge of the Church?

Church Questions

Who's in Charge of the Church?

Sam Emadi

:: CROSSWAY®

WHEATON, ILLINOIS

Trade paperback ISBN: 978-1-4335-7871-7
ePub ISBN: 978-1-4335-7874-8
PDF ISBN: 978-1-4335-7872-4
Mobipocket ISBN: 978-1-4335-7873-1

Library of Congress Cataloging-in-Publication Data

Names: Emadi, Sam, author.
Title: Who's in charge of the church? / Sam Emadi.
Description: Wheaton, Illinois : Crossway, [2022] | Series: Church questions | Includes bibliographical references and index.
Identifiers: LCCN 2021048773 (print) | LCCN 2021048774 (ebook) | ISBN 9781433578717 (trade paperback) | ISBN 9781433578724 (pdf) | ISBN 9781433578731 (mobi) | ISBN 9781433578748 (epub)
Subjects: LCSH: Church polity. | Church.
Classification: LCC BV647.3 .E43 2022 (print) | LCC BV647.3 (ebook) | DDC 262--dc23/eng/20211221
LC record available at https://lccn.loc.gov/2021048773
LC ebook record available at https://lccn.loc.gov/2021048774

Crossway is a publishing ministry of Good News Publishers.

BP		31	30	29	28	27	26	25	24	23	22
15	14	13	12	11	10	9	8	7	6	5	4	3	2	1

And he gave the apostles, the prophets,
the evangelists, the shepherds and teachers,
to equip the saints for the work of ministry,
for building up the body of Christ.

Ephesians 4:11–12

Does this story sound familiar?

Unity Church met for its quarterly business meeting. On the agenda was a motion to use a portion of the church's budget surplus to re-upholster the pews in the sanctuary. Church members could feel the room tense up as a deacon brought the motion to the floor. After all, Old Man Miller's grandfather built those pews more than a hundred years ago. One even had a plaque on the armrest commemorating its installation. He couldn't believe how ungrateful people had become. Frankly, the whole conversation seemed disrespectful.

But some younger folks didn't understand all the drama. The church needed to get with the times, they said. Young people wouldn't join the church if it continued to look—and smell—like a monument to the 1930s.

The moderator bravely asked if there was any discussion. What followed was more like a cage-fight than a consideration. Nearly thirty minutes later, the pastor's wife was in tears, the church had nearly split between the "new-pewers" and the "old-pewers," and the motion was tabled. Everyone went home thinking the worst about everyone else.

The whole episode smacked of disorder and chaos. Anyone on the outside looking in would have surely asked, "Who's in charge here?"

———

Or does this story sound familiar?

Jen had been a member at Connection Church for years. She recently reconnected with her old high school friend Heather who had started coming to church with her. At first, it seemed like Heather became a Christian. She had a clear understanding of the gospel and her speech was brimming with Christian lingo. She was even baptized and joined the church. She came consistently to Sunday morning worship and started attending a small group and meeting up with some ladies in the church for a Bible study.

But over time, the church started to see less and less of Heather. She stopped attending small group. Her ladies' Bible study couldn't get her to respond to text messages. Eventually, she stopped showing up on Sundays. Before long, Jen and some other members started talking about how "the pastors let her slip through the cracks." The pastors, on the other hand, wished more folks would have reached out to Heather as they saw her slipping away.

Surely someone should have stepped in and pursued her. But who was responsible for that? Who's in charge around here?

———

The above stories are fictional, but I'm sure you've got some real and perhaps even painful stories where it just seemed like no one in the church really had their hand on the steering wheel. Perhaps you've had a few moments where you've left a business meeting or a worship service asking, "Who's in charge here?"

That's an important question. And, believe it or not, the Bible actually gives *a lot* of attention to it. In his infinite wisdom, Jesus has ordered the church to reflect his own merciful and gracious rule. He cares deeply about the question, "Who's in charge here?" because he created the church, he loves the church, and he wants the church to be united and peaceful.

Thankfully, our Savior gave the church some pretty clear marching orders about who in the church has authority and what exactly they have the authority to do. That's what this little booklet is about.

This topic may seem niche, maybe even a bit boring. A book on "church polity"? *Bleh.*

But stay with me for at least the next couple of pages. I think you may find that questions even as mundane as who should be choosing the color of the church carpet actually reveal some glorious truths about what a local church is, what Jesus created it to do, and how all of this boring talk about church polity has some pretty massive implications for your life.

Just two quick notes before we get going.

First, different denominations and theological traditions give different answers to the question, "Who's in charge at church?" So you should know up front that what I'm going to be saying is a uniquely Baptist answer to that question. Of course, I believe this "Baptist" answer ultimately because I think it comes from the Bible. So throughout this book I'll be appealing to Scripture, not Baptist tradition, to make my case.

Second, every church, even the most mature, well-ordered congregation, sometimes struggles with disunity and hurt feelings between members. We hurt each other not ultimately because of some disorder in church structure but because we're still sinners with a healthy dose of selfishness bound up in our hearts. So, no—a biblically ordered church can't stop every divisive word, unchecked bitterness, or act of disunity. But a biblically ordered church does have the means to deal with these sins in a healthy, redemptive way and in a way that keeps disunity from spreading like gangrene. Good church order is like a helmet that you can throw on top of a disunity grenade. The grenade still explodes but the helmet helps contain the shrapnel.

Who's in Charge of *What*?

It turns out, when we ask the question, "Who's in charge around here?" the Bible gives us both a simple answer and a complicated one.

The Simple Answer

We'll start with the simple answer first: Jesus is in charge of your church.

See, I told you that was simple.

Let's elaborate a little. Jesus is the Lord of the church. He established the church and rules over it by his word. What is that word? Scripture. In Scripture, we find the words of the King governing the church. He tells us the mission of the church (Matt. 28:18–20). He tells us how we should relate to one another (John 13:34–35). He tells us how to keep the church pure (Matt. 18:15–20). He tells us who should do the preaching and teaching (1 Tim. 2:12; 3:2) and what the content of that preaching and teaching should be (2 Tim. 4:1–2).

Jesus sets the rules. He orders our life together.

Scripture is the voice of the King governing his subjects and ordering his people according to his commands.

So who runs the church? Jesus does. He's the King—the Lord of the church.

The Complicated Answer

At this point you're probably thinking, *Well, that's a nice Sunday School answer, but Jesus doesn't exactly show up at the members' meeting and tell us whether we should add a skylight to the building or lay new carpet in the foyer.* Of course, that's true. But Jesus did give instructions on how the church should make these types of practical decisions, how it can care for its members, and who's ultimately responsible for different aspects of church life.

So here comes the complicated answer. When we ask, "Who's in charge at church?" we first have to ask, "in charge of *what*?" You see, Jesus has authorized different offices in the church to do different things. Sometimes, the Bible tells *the whole church* (meaning all the members of the church) that they have to do something. Other times, the Bible tells the elders of the church (also called *pastors*) that they have to do something. Scripture gives members and elders different job descriptions.

So let's take a minute and see what Jesus says about what the *whole church* should do and what *the elders* should do. This may feel like a bit of deep dive into some theological minutiae, but stay with me. In the end, you'll discover all sorts of practical implications, not just about how a church makes decisions but about how *you* should live out your devotion to Jesus in the context of a local church.

"Let them call for "The Elders" James

Who's in Charge at Church?
The Whole Church

Let's get to the bottom line. Who's in charge at church? The answer is the *whole church*. The whole congregation has the responsibility for its health, its preaching, and its membership. *All the members* together are responsible.

Where do we see this in the Bible? Well, are you ready to jump into some deep theology? Great! Let's first talk about Batman.

Maybe you've never thought about it, but Batman can teach us a lot about our responsibilities at church as members.

Surprised? Well, think about it for a moment. Batman's just an ordinary person, a regular guy roaming the streets of Gotham in a batsuit bringing justice to criminals. He doesn't have special Kryptonian DNA like Superman. He was never injected with a super-soldier serum like Captain America. But when the Dark Knight sees the bat symbol light up the sky, he suits up and gets to work *guarding* the city of Gotham. He's an ordinary man with an extraordinary task.[1]

What does any of this have to do with your role as a church member? Well, quite a bit. Church members have been commissioned by God to *guard the gospel*. That's what *the whole church* is in charge of. That task may seem like something that should be entrusted to spiritual superheroes. But God in his wisdom has put that responsibility on normal church members like you.

Let's see this in the Bible—specifically in Matthew 16 and 18.

In Matthew 16, Jesus asks the apostles who they think he is. Peter pipes up first: "You are the Christ, the Son of the living God" (Matt. 16:16). Jesus's reply is a stunning statement not just about Peter but about all those who imitate Peter's faith:

> And Jesus answered him, "Blessed are you, Simon Bar-Jonah! For flesh and blood has not revealed this to you, but my Father who is in heaven. And I tell you, you are Peter, and on this rock I will build my church, and the gates of hell shall not prevail against it.

I will give you the keys of the kingdom of heaven, and whatever you bind on earth shall be bound in heaven, and whatever you loose on earth shall be loosed in heaven." (Matt. 16:17–19)

Jesus is going to build his church on Peter—on the confessor and his confession. But more than that, Jesus is going to give Peter and the other apostles the "keys of the kingdom of heaven." What do these keys do? In short, they have the authority to be heaven's spokesmen like Jesus.

Perhaps even more remarkable, however, is that Jesus gives this same authority ("the keys of the kingdom of heaven") not just to the apostles but to local churches of ordinary men and women who believe in Jesus. How do we know? Because the same language Jesus uses here in Matthew 16 shows up again in Matthew 18, but he's applying it to a group of people *other than* the apostles.

If your brother sins against you, go and tell him his fault, between you and him alone.

If he listens to you, you have gained your brother. But if he does not listen, take one or two others along with you, that every charge may be established by the evidence of two or three witnesses. If he refuses to listen to them, tell it to the church. And if he refuses to listen even to the church, let him be to you as a Gentile and a tax collector. Truly, I say to you, whatever you bind on earth shall be bound in heaven, and whatever you loose on earth shall be loosed in heaven. Again I say to you, if two of you agree on earth about anything they ask, it will be done for them by my Father in heaven. For where two or three are gathered in my name, there am I among them. (Matt. 18:15–20)

In Matthew 18, we see that local churches (the members as one body, not just the leadership) must guard the gospel by overseeing one another's membership in the kingdom of God. They do this as a single, assembled body. Notice Jesus makes that point clearly when he talks about "two or three" (that is to say a group of people) "gathered" in his name and with his authority. The local church, then, is the spokespeople of heaven. They do that work by overseeing a person's *life* and his or her *confession* to ensure that it's consistent with the gospel. Each church member must *guard the gospel* both in his or her life and in the lives of fellow church members.

You may be asking, "Why would Christ do this? Why would he put such an important responsibility into the hands of ordinary Christians?" Well, as it turns out, every ordinary Christian has been given extraordinary grace. According to Scripture, all genuine Christians have the law of God written on their hearts (Jer. 31:33). All Christians know God (Jer. 31:34). All Christians have the Spirit of God residing in them, sanctifying them, and causing them to grow into maturity in Christ (Rom. 8:9; Phil. 1:6).

We may be ordinary Christians, but there's nothing ordinary about Christians. We're all products of God's supernatural, redemptive work of grace. The reason Christ commissions local church members to guard the gospel is because every Christian has been equipped to guard the gospel. Who we are (those who believe the gospel) gives rise to what we're called to do (guard the gospel).

How exactly do we do this?

Well, the answer requires more than enumerating a to-do list. Instead, we need to recognize that every aspect of the Christian life should contribute to this overarching commission.

- We affirm others as fellow church members by baptism and the Lord's Supper. Through baptism a congregation receives new believers into membership. It's how the church tells someone, "Hey, based on the credibility of your profession of faith, we understand you to be a Christian." Then in the Lord's Supper we partake of the same meal as one body, essentially telling one another, "Hey, we still understand you to be a Christian."
- We disciple others as a way of guarding the purity of the gospel in their lives.
- We ask others to disciple us to ensure that we contribute to the church's health and can

faithfully carry out our responsibilities as Christians.

- We bar from communion those who live out of accord with the gospel or confess a gospel contrary to Scripture. This is what Jesus taught in Matthew 18, the passage we read earlier. If someone refuses to continue to repent of ongoing sin, then the church can't continue affirming the credibility of that person's profession of faith. After all, repentance and faith are what make someone a Christian (Mark 1:15).
- We clearly articulate our gospel profession by affirming a biblical statement of faith.
- We expel false teachers from our midst, even firing them from the church if their message is inconsistent with the biblical gospel (Gal. 1:8).

In all of these ways and more, we guard the gospel and govern the church.

You can summarize all of this biblical data into three simple points. The whole church is responsible for its (1) membership, (2) discipline, and (3) doctrine.

Let's walk through each of those points.

First, the congregation is in charge of the church's members. This means that the whole church needs to care for and disciple its members. In other words, it's not just the job of the pastors or church staff to make sure that people are growing. Additionally, the whole congregation has to receive new members into church fellowship. The pastors and staff can't just "willy-nilly" add someone to the membership rolls. The whole church has to agree on adding someone to the membership.

Second, the congregation is responsible for discipline. When a member of the church stops following Jesus by refusing to repent of sin, the church has the responsibility to lovingly pursue that person and call him or her to repentance. If that wayward brother or sister fails to respond like a Christian, then the church must "discipline" that person from the fellowship. "Discipline" means that the congregation removes that person from membership, tells that person that they are no longer confident in his or her profession of faith, and no longer welcomes him or her to celebrate the Lord's Supper.

Finally, the church is responsible for its doctrine. The whole church must define what it believes the Bible teaches and hold one another to that standard. The church also has to appoint its own elders—those capable of teaching the Bible faithfully (1 Tim. 5:17–20). They also have the responsibility to remove from leadership false teachers who are leading the congregation astray (Gal. 1:8).

At this point, we need to push a little deeper. I've just argued that the congregation is responsible to care for the church's membership, discipline, and doctrine. But I don't want you to assume that that responsibility is limited to *events* in the church's life, like a members' meeting. In other words, *if* final authority over "membership, discipline, and doctrine" just means the "vote" cast by a congregation to bring someone in, put someone out, or affirm a statement of faith, then it's easy to see why you may feel like a church's polity has very little to do with your day-to-day life.

But think about it a bit more. If a congregation receives someone into membership, then that congregation now bears the responsibility of overseeing, encouraging, and discipling that member long after the members' meeting ends. The congregation owns that person's day-to-day faithfulness as part of its stewardship. Authority to bind and loose are not expressed only in the one-time events of receiving or dismissing people from the church.

In other words, voting to receive a member is more like getting married than casting a ballot for the next elected official. Marriage includes the *event* of the wedding, but this event inaugurates the day-to-day commitments and responsibilities that the two parties now bear to one another. When a congregation receives someone into membership, that congregation takes on the day-to-day duty of meeting with, praying for, and discipling that member throughout the week and in the corporate gathering. When a congregation puts someone out of membership, that congregation has the day-to-day duty of treating that person as a tax-collector and calling him or her to repentance. Congregational authority over membership and discipline therefore are not merely one-time events but daily responsibilities.

Similarly, the congregation's authority over the church's doctrine isn't merely expressed in the one-time vote affirming the church's statement of faith. That's certainly part of the equation, but the congregation must now take that doctrine and push it into the nooks and crannies of church life and into the lives of the members. Is a member struggling to believe that God cares for him? Then it's your job to remind him of the truths of the gospel and that God always reigns with providential care over his children. Is a member complacent toward the lost? Maybe she's beginning to lose sight of what the Bible teaches about hell. Do you see someone in your church discouraged because he's trying to earn favor with God through his own works? Remind him of the truth of justification by faith alone and that our standing before God is rooted in Christ's righteousness and not our own. You guard the church's doctrine, not just by affirming the church's confession but by encouraging everyone in the church to live in light of those truths, in the good times and in the bad.

So, who's in charge at church? The whole congregation, with each member playing his or her part. If someone starts to slip away from the fellowship, church members should go after that person. If the pastor starts teaching false doctrine, church members should remove him from the pulpit. If someone wants to join the church, church members should have an opportunity to hear about the person's conversion and understanding of the gospel before they receive him or her into fellowship. If someone is living in unrepentant sin, church members need to decide to discipline that person from the congregation.

The church is in charge of guarding the gospel: making sure that each member continues to live a life shaped by the gospel and that the church continues to teach and preach the gospel.

Who's in Charge at Church? The Elders

I know what some of you are thinking: this sounds like democratic chaos. If the whole congregation has to make decisions, then does that mean the congregation has to vote on *everything*?

- If the church starts a new Sunday school class, does the congregation need to meet to vote on who should teach it?
- If the church puts new carpet in the sanctuary, does each member need to give input on what color it should be?
- Does the whole church need to create the church budget from scratch each year?

Thankfully, the Bible shows us that the church doesn't have to gather to vote on *every* conceivable issue. Instead, Scripture teaches that another group of people in the church are also responsible for the church's life and ministry. That group of people is called the elders.

In the Bible, elders (also called pastors) are commissioned by Jesus to give leadership to the congregation. Peter gives a good summary of the elders' job description in 1 Peter 5:1–4:

> So I exhort the elders among you, as a fellow elder and a witness of the sufferings

of Christ, as well as a partaker in the glory
that is going to be revealed: shepherd the
flock of God that is among you, exercis-
ing oversight, not under compulsion, but
willingly, as God would have you; not for
shameful gain, but eagerly; not domineer-
ing over those in your charge, but being
examples to the flock. And when the chief
Shepherd appears, you will receive the un-
fading crown of glory.

Did you notice all the *authority* and *responsibility* words that are in that paragraph? Elders
must "shepherd," "exercise oversight," and serve
as "examples" to the whole congregation. Elders
have a very real authority in the local church.
In fact, the author of Hebrews makes this same
point but from the opposite perspective, encouraging church members to submit to the elders
over them.

Obey your leaders and submit to them, for
they are keeping watch over your souls, as
those who will have to give an account. Let
them do this with joy and not with groan-

ing, for that would be of no advantage to you. (Heb. 13:17)

Elders must lead the congregation. A congregation must follow the leadership of its elders.

But *how* exactly do elders lead the church? In the following three ways:

First, elders teach the Bible to the church. The primary thing that distinguishes elders from the rest of the congregation and from deacons is that elders are "able to teach" (1 Tim. 3:2). In fact, that's their primary role in the life of the church. Listen to how Paul describes an elder's job:

> Until I come, devote yourself to the public reading of Scripture, to exhortation, to teaching. Do not neglect the gift you have, which was given you by prophecy when the council of elders laid their hands on you. Practice these things, immerse yourself in them, so that all may see your progress. Keep a close watch on yourself and on the teaching. Persist in this, for by so doing you will save both yourself and your hearers. (1 Tim. 4:13–16)

In fact, elders aren't only commanded to positively promote sound teaching, they're also commissioned to protect the church from false teaching. Consider Paul's warning to the Ephesian elders:

> I know that after my departure fierce wolves will come in among you, not sparing the flock; and from among your own selves will arise men speaking twisted things, to draw away the disciples after them. Therefore be alert, remembering that for three years I did not cease night or day to admonish every one with tears. (Acts 20:29–31)

Elders must exercise their authority in the congregation by teaching the word. By teaching, the elders equip church members to obey Jesus and carry out their responsibilities.

Second, the elders model obedience to the Bible. Have you ever read the qualifications for being an elder in 1 Timothy 3? They're striking because they're so ordinary:

> The saying is trustworthy: If anyone aspires to the office of overseer, he desires a noble

task. Therefore an overseer must be above reproach, the husband of one wife, sober-minded, self-controlled, respectable, hospitable, able to teach, not a drunkard, not violent but gentle, not quarrelsome, not a lover of money. He must manage his own household well, with all dignity keeping his children submissive, for if someone does not know how to manage his own household, how will he care for God's church? He must not be a recent convert, or he may become puffed up with conceit and fall into the condemnation of the devil. Moreover, he must be well thought of by outsiders, so that he may not fall into disgrace, into a snare of the devil. (1 Tim. 3:1–7)

Shouldn't this list characterize every Christian? Well, that's kind of the point. Elders are supposed to be *good-example* Christians—models of the Christian life for all who belong to the church. Peter makes the same point in the passage we read earlier when he tells elders to be "examples to the flock" (1 Pet. 5:3). Elders lead the church by modeling obedience to Jesus.

Finally, elders give oversight to the congregation. They must make decisions for the church and, as we just read in Hebrews 13:17, God commands the congregation to submit to those decisions and follow them. Scripture teaches this idea not only in the fact that elders are sometimes called "overseers" (Phil. 1:1; 1 Tim. 3:1–2; Titus 1:7) but also in passages like 1 Timothy 5:17:

> Let the elders who rule well be considered worthy of double honor, especially those who labor in preaching and teaching.

The elders must "rule" in the church. Obviously they must do so with love and care, but Scripture invests a church's elders with a very real authority to make decisions regarding the affairs of the church.

In short: elders lead the congregation. You might even say they're the ones "in charge" at church.

How Do These Two Ideas Fit Together?

At this point you might be scratching your head. It seems like the Bible is teaching two contradictory ideas. The congregation is in charge *and* the elders are in charge. The congregation is responsible for the church's life, but the congregation must also submit to the leadership of the elders.

So how does this all work together? Thankfully, the Bible helps us answer this question. One of the most helpful passages that discusses how elders and the congregation relate is Ephesians 4:11–12:

> And he gave the apostles, the prophets, the evangelists, the shepherds and teachers, to equip the saints for the work of ministry, for building up the body of Christ.

Do you see it? "Shepherds and teachers" (that is, the elders) equip the church to do the work of the ministry. The elders *teach* and *model* healthy ministry, and the congregation *does* ministry. The elders lead, and the congregation follows. Elders teach—by word, by example—and the congregation imitates their faith.

My friend Jonathan Leeman often likens the relationship between the elders and the congregation to an exercise class. The elders are like the exercise teacher standing up in front of the class saying, "Look at how I do this stretch. You really have to make sure you keep your toes straight. OK, now you do it too." The class needs the teacher to model for them how to work out properly.

It's the same with elders and congregations. The elders say, "Here's how we obey Jesus. See what the Bible says about this? See how I follow Jesus this way? Great, now you do it too."

Theologians call this type of church polity "elder-led congregationalism." You may want to remember that term because I'm going to use it in a few places in the rest of this book.

The elders don't *usurp* the congregation's authority, they *equip* the congregation to exercise its authority rightly. That's how the congregation can be "in charge" and yet still "submit" to leadership. The leadership says, "The Bible says you should take this action," and the congregation says, "We'll follow your lead and your biblical instruction. Let's take that action."

In fact one place in Scripture where we see this principle in action is 1 Corinthians 5 in a case of church discipline. In that text, Paul tells the Corinthian church that he has already passed "judgment" on the man requiring discipline (v. 3). But Paul's judgment (even though he was an apostle) didn't remove the man from the church. Instead, Paul wanted the church to remove the unrepentant man from fellowship. They must "judge" the man as well (v. 12). Do you see the logic? Paul is acting like an elder. He's telling the church "I've taken this action, now you need to do it too."

Before we move on to the next section, let me add that this pattern of elders leading and congregation following isn't restricted merely to how a church makes decisions about membership or other matters of church life. This principle applies to the whole Christian life. God gives church elders so they can tell church members, "Watch how I love my wife and children; watch how I endure suffering; watch how I live generously with my money; watch how I evangelize. Now you do it too."

I said at the beginning of this book that what we believe about church polity has some massive implications for how you think about the Christian life. I hope you're beginning to see why that's the case. Elder-led congregationalism isn't just about how a church makes decisions, it's actually God's discipleship program for the church. Elders teach and model how to love Christ and care for others so that the whole congregation can learn how to love and care for one another.

Steering Wheels and Emergency Brakes

My lowest grade in high school was driver's education—a point which comes as no surprise to my wife, mind you. I miserably failed the exam that required me to label different parts of the engine. Despite my ignorance of an automobile's anatomy, I'm now going to venture into an illustration that requires at least some rudimentary knowledge of how a car works.

You can think about the relationship between the authority of the elders and the authority of the congregation like the relationship between a steering wheel and an emergency brake. The elders have their hands on the steering wheel. They're navigating the car and its passengers through winding, sometimes turbulent streets of this world.

The congregation, meanwhile, sits in the passenger seat, trusting the elders to get them to the right destination. But if the congregation decides that the elders have made a seriously wrong turn or that they are about to run the church off a cliff, the congregation can pull the emergency brake. Pulling that brake is a fairly radical action. After all, how many times have you used yours? But by pulling that emergency brake, the congregation is essentially saying, "We need new drivers because these aren't headed in the right direction."

Some Practical Implications

This may sound like a lot of procedural nitpicking, but the implications of the Bible's design for the church are actually profound and affect far more than your next members' meeting. Let me lay out a few practical implications.

First, your church doesn't need to vote on *everything*.

The only things the congregation *must* vote on are matters directly pertaining to the church's membership, discipline, or doctrine. So, is your church receiving new members? Then the assembled congregation needs to take that action. Are you excommunicating someone from your church's fellowship? Then your whole church needs to take that action. Are you hiring a pastor or changing your church's statement of faith (matters pertaining to doctrine)? Then your whole church needs to agree on that action.

Remember, the congregation (not just the elders) is responsible to guard the gospel and guard one another. Every time your church receives someone into membership, you're not just saying you believe that person to have a credible faith in the gospel, you're making a commitment to take responsibility for that person. You're essentially saying to that new member, "We're going to watch over your soul and come alongside you so that you keep on trusting Christ, keep on repenting of sin, and keep on holding to sound doctrine." You're not just voting to put a name on the church membership roll, you're committing to building a relationship with that person for the sake of encouraging him or her to persevere in devotion to Jesus.

What about all the other stuff in church life? Well, you can leave that to the elders and submit to their wisdom.

The whole church doesn't need to deliberate on the color of the new carpet in the foyer. The whole church doesn't need to take action on whether the next potluck should be at 5 or 6 p.m. The whole church doesn't need to vote on whether the pastoral intern should read eight books or nine. Those issues should just be left in the hands of the elders.

Sometimes, the elders may choose to delegate some of those decisions to other groups in the church like a staff member or the deacons of the church who assist the elders and care for the practical needs of the congregation. Those groups, however, still serve under the general oversight and leadership of the elders.

Second, invite your pastors into your life.

Their job is to teach you how to be a Christian and how to carry out your responsibility in ensuring the church stays healthy. That's tough to do if you're constantly keeping them at arm's length. So avail yourself of your pastors. Let them know what you're thinking about and how you're doing spiritually. Ask for their advice on life decisions. Be a sheep that's easy to shepherd.

Further, ask your elders about the church. Do you have concerns? Are you troubled about something going on in the body? Let them know and ask how you can be a part of the solution. Don't complain or gossip but invite their instruction and let them explain why they're leading the church the way they are. You might not agree with everything they say. That's OK. You still need to submit to their judgments and trust the wisdom God is giving them, even if you might see things a little differently. That, of course, isn't always easy. Submission to authority is hard. But it's possible to follow godly leaders, even when we disagree with them, because our submission to them is ultimately rooted in our submission to Jesus. We submit to elders and obey Hebrews 13:17 for Jesus's sake.

Third, clearly understanding your job and the elders' job is a great way to preserve the unity of the church.

So often disunity emerges from folks trying to put their hands into matters that don't really belong to them. Grabs for power usually create fights for power. But when everyone knows their job description and *who* is responsible for *what*, then we have a much better shot at preserving the unity of the church.

In fact, let's revisit some of those "church fights" we mentioned at the beginning of the book and see if we can't apply some of what we've learned to resolving those situations.

Remember Unity Baptist Church and their fight over whether to reupholster the pews? One group wanted to honor the past. Another wanted to look forward to the future. Well, does any of this *actually* affect the church's membership, discipline, and doctrine? Not really. The church's furniture doesn't hinder the congregation's ability to receive new members into the church or care for the members' spiritual well-being—and it certainly doesn't affect the church's gospel doctrine. So in the end, this is just a matter of wisdom—a decision best left to the elders (or to someone they may delegate to care for the matter), and the church should follow their lead. The elders might not make the decision *you* would have made, but you have to trust that they're concerned about the whole church, making the best decision they can, and perhaps working with some information that you don't have.

Remember Heather at Connection Church? She started well but after a season "slipped through the cracks." Who should have gone after her? And what should the church do now? Well, the members, fueled by the regular teaching of the elders, should have pursued her. They should have reminded her that true Christians don't "forsake the assembly" (Heb. 10:25). They should have called her to repentance. Of course, the elders should be involved in that process, too, but the responsibility wasn't *only* on their shoulders. Now that Heather has resolutely abandoned the church and rebuffed any efforts at rejoining the gathering, the elders should show from Scripture that the congregation has the responsibility to "discipline" her from the church and no longer affirm the credibility of her profession.

As you can see, the whole thing is a glorious design for the church's good and for the edification of the saints. The elders lead and teach, the congregation responds, submits, and takes action.

Imagine you invite a friend from church to coffee. As the conversation turns to church life, her body language expresses a little bit of agitation. "I just don't understand why we're not fixing the walkway on the side of the building. I mean, that's where most people park. I'm sure it's a huge turnoff to visitors!"

What should you do in that situation? I would suggest you might want to remind your friend of everyone's job description. "Yeah, that walkway does need some work. But remember the elders explained that they thought the church needed to buy pew Bibles to give away to visitors and repair the air conditioning in the sanctuary instead. It might not be what we would have decided, but we do need to follow our leaders. And at the end of the day, our job is to care for members and value good doctrine. We can do that with or without that walkway."

Knowing our roles and following our leaders helps us maintain the unity of the church. If you have a congregation that's constantly at odds with the elders, you either have ungodly elders not worth following or an ungodly congregation unwilling to follow.

Fourth, foster a culture of trust for godly leadership in your church.

Don't set yourself up as an independent review board for every decision the elders make. After all, your church established these leaders in the first place, so offer them the trust they need to lead the congregation well. Recognize that while the elders do need to inform the congregation well enough so that it can make wise decisions, they may have good reasons for not telling the congregation everything they know about a particular situation going on in the life the church.

A Few Final Questions

What If I've Lost Trust in My Elders?

If you're in a place where you can't trust your elders, you should probably leave your church. If they consistently make decisions that you consider profoundly unwise or even put the gospel at risk, it's time to transfer your membership elsewhere. Not every elder and not every elder board *deserves* your trust.

But before you do, examine your heart, ask for counsel, and honestly assess whether you're being suspicious and unsubmissive. The problem, after all, might not be your elders, it might be your unwillingness to trust them. But if you come to a place where you don't think your elders deserve trust, it's best to peaceably leave and find a place with leadership you can follow.

What If I Trust My Elders but Just Can't Vote in Favor of a Proposal They're Making?

Maybe you do generally trust your elders, but they're about to bring a motion up at the next members' meeting that you're having a really tough time supporting.

For instance, imagine the elders propose a budget to the church which significantly reduces the church's giving to your favorite missions organization and instead designates that money to some building renovations. In your mind, this restructuring of the church's budget is unwise. You're having a tough time getting on board.

What do you do?

First, find an elder and make your concerns known to him. Don't come into the conversation ready to accuse. Ask lots of questions and be willing to listen. Follow James's command: "Let every person be quick to hear, slow to speak" (James 1:19). Too many church members ignore this first step and let disagreement and dissatisfaction fester in their hearts.

Second, have a teachable spirit and a posture of humility. As you listen to the elders, give their reasons a fair hearing. After all, the book of Proverbs commends this approach as the path of wisdom:

- "The way of a fool is right in his own eyes, but a wise man listens to advice" (Prov. 12:15).
- "A fool takes no pleasure in understanding, but only in expressing his opinion" (Prov. 18:2).
- "If one gives an answer before he hears, it is his folly and shame" (Prov. 18:13).

You may still decide that you would have made a different judgment. But at least be willing to grant that the elders' decision was reasonable and thoughtful.

Third, ask yourself, "Is this a wisdom issue or a gospel issue?" If the elders have made a decision that puts the gospel at risk, you're not only free to oppose them, you *must* do so. Never follow an elder into sin or into practices that deny a true understanding of the gospel.

More often, however, you'll probably just disagree with your elders about a matter of wisdom. Wisdom issues don't put the gospel at stake; they're just matters of *good*, *better*, and *best*.

- Should the church give to missions organization A or missions organization B?
- Should the church use its budget surplus to give more to missions or should they use that money to service the mortgage on the building?
- Should the church hire a counseling pastor or an outreach pastor?
- Should the church repair the parking lot or the roof?

Questions like these don't put the gospel at risk. On any issue of wisdom, I would encourage you to submit cheerfully to your elders and follow their leadership, even if you harbor a different opinion.

Finally, if the elders are going to ask the congregation to vote on a particular wisdom issue, and you come to the place where you cannot in good conscience vote in favor of the elders' proposal, consider abstaining from the vote.

If you're conscience bound to vote against it, then let your elders know in advance that you intend to vote against their proposal. And then do your best to promote the unity of the church.

Don't gossip or slander. Live out your disagreement in the spirit of Titus 3:1–2: "Remind them to be submissive to rulers and authorities, to be obedient, to be ready for every good work, to speak evil of no one, to avoid quarreling, to be gentle, and to show perfect courtesy toward all people."

Let's Do the Job

The local church is a special place, one worth preserving and defending. Paul writes in Ephesians 3:10 that "through the church the manifold wisdom of God might now be made known to the rulers and authorities in the heavenly places." Asking questions like "who's in charge at church?" may feel cold and procedural, but something of the wisdom and glory of God is made known as we answer these sorts of questions.

Ultimately, we all have a job to do.

- If you're an elder—teach, model, and lead your church well. Don't usurp authority but equip the congregation to use its authority well.

- If you're a church member—listen to your elders, submit to their leadership, and follow their example. Yet you have a job to do. You're in charge of protecting fellow church members and upholding the gospel in your congregation. Let your elders equip you for that task so you can do it well.

Fellow Christian, let's embrace the responsibilities put in front of us and protect the gospel. Let's do the job Jesus assigned us so that "the manifold wisdom of God" might be made known to the world.

Recommended Resources

Jonathan Leeman, *Don't Fire Your Church Members: The Case for Congregationalism* (Nashville, TN: B&H Academic, 2016).

Jonathan Leeman, *Understanding the Congregation's Authority* (Nashville, TN: B&H, 2016).

Jeramie Rinne, *Church Elders: How to Shepherd God's People Like Jesus* (Wheaton, IL: Crossway, 2014).

Notes

1. A significant portion of this section is adapted from Sam Emadi, "Be Like Batman: Guard the Gospel" 9Marks website, March 30, 2021, https://www.9marks.org/article/be-like-batman-guard-the-gospel/?lang=de.

Scripture Index

IX 9Marks

Building Healthy Churches

9Marks exists to equip church leaders with a biblical vision and practical resources for displaying God's glory to the nations through healthy churches.

To that end, we want to see churches characterized by these nine marks of health:

1. Expositional Preaching
2. Gospel Doctrine
3. A Biblical Understanding of Conversion and Evangelism
4. Biblical Church Membership
5. Biblical Church Discipline
6. A Biblical Concern for Discipleship and Growth
7. Biblical Church Leadership
8. A Biblical Understanding of the Practice of Prayer
9. A Biblical Understanding and Practice of Missions

Find all our Crossway titles and other resources at 9Marks.org.

John Onwuchekwa — Church Questions

Sam Emadi — Church Questions

Mark Dever — Church Questions

...el Like ...o Church?

...sen

Does God Love Everyone?
Matt McCullough — Church Questions

How Can I Find Someone to Disciple Me?
J. Garrett Kell — Church Questions

How Can Women T... the Local...
Keri Folmar — Church Questions

...ized?

...on

How Can Our Church Find a Faithful Pastor?
Mark Dever — Church Questions

Is It Loving to Practice Church Discipline?
Jonathan Leeman — Church Questions

How Can I Love Ch... Members... Different...
Jonathan & Andy N... — Church Questions

IX 9Marks Church Questions

Providing ordinary Christians with sound and accessible biblical teaching by answering common questions about church life.

For more information, visit crossway.org.